# A POCKET GUIDE TO
# Correct English

# A POCKET GUIDE TO
# Correct English
## Second Edition

**Michael Temple**

## BARRON'S

**BARRON'S EDUCATIONAL SERIES, INC.**
New York/London/Toronto/Sydney

Second U.S. Edition (revised) 1990 by Barron's Educational Series, Inc.

First U.S. Edition 1982 by Barron's Educational Series, Inc.

© Michael Temple 1978

British edition published by John Murray (Publishers) Ltd.

First published 1978, reprinted (revised) 1979, 1980

The title of the British edition is:
### A POCKET GUIDE TO WRITTEN ENGLISH
by Michael Temple

*All inquiries should be addressed to:*
Barron's Educational Series, Inc.
250 Wireless Boulevard
Hauppauge, New York 11788


International Standard Book No. 0-8120-4285-9

PRINTED IN THE UNITED STATES OF AMERICA

12   590   9876543

# Contents

# **Acknowledgments**

I am grateful to my wife and colleagues for their valuable assistance and to my pupils, past and present, without whose errors I could not have written this booklet.

# 1 Spelling

(See also **Words often confused,** p. 25)

## General

Wide, attentive reading will obviously help with spelling, as with all matters of expression. Careful pronunciation and grouping words in families may also help. It is a good idea to underline that part of a word which gives you trouble. Always check with a dictionary or the list of commonly misspelled words if you are at all uncertain.

It is best to learn a few spellings at a time and to know the rules (see pages 17 to 24).

**(a)** Study the word carefully and pronounce it.

**(b)** Shut your eyes and try to picture the word.

**(c)** Check the spelling.

**(d)** Write it down from memory.

**(e)** Check it carefully.

## ALPHABETICAL LIST OF THE MOST COMMONLY MISSPELLED WORDS

### (See Chapter 2 for words like *affect/effect* and *council/counsel*)

abbreviate
abhorrent
abominable
abscess
absence
abysmal
abyss
academically
accelerate
accelerator
accessible
accidentally
acclaim
acclamation
accommodate
accommodation
accompaniment
accompany
accomplice
accomplish
accurately
aching
achievement
acknowledg(e)ment
acquaintance
acquiesce
acquire
acquisition

acquit(ted)
acreage
across
adaptation
address
adequate
adjacent
adjourn
admission
admittance
admitted
advantageous
advertisement
aerial
aggravate
aggregate
aggression
agreeable
aisle (in a church)
alcohol
allege
allegiance
alleviate
allot(ted)
allotment
all right (2 words)
a lot (2 words)
although

amateur
among
analysis, analyses
ancestor
ancestry
ancillary
annihilate
announce
annual(ly)
anonymous
antidote
apartment
appalling
apparatus
apparent
appeal(ing)
appear(ance)
approach
appropriate
approximately
arctic
arguing
argument
arithmetic
arrangement
arrest
arrival
arrogant
article
ascertain
assassinate
assault
associate
athletics
atmosphere
attached

attempt
attitude
attract
author
automatically
autumn
autumnal
awesome
awful(ly)
awkward

bachelor
balance
balloon
balloted
banisters
bankruptcy
barrenness
basically
bath (n.)
bathe (vb.)
baton
battalion
bazaar
beautiful(ly)
beggar
beginning
behavior
beige
belief
believe
bench, benches
benefactor
benefited
bereaved
besiege

bicycle
blatant
boisterous
bouillon
boycott
brief
broken
budgeted
building
burglar
business
busily

calculator
calendar
calf, calves
camouflage
campaign
cannibal
canoeing
careers
careful(ly)
careless
Caribbean
caricature
carpentry
catastrophe(s)
category
caterpillar
ceiling
cellar
cemetery
century, centuries
changeable
chaos
character

characteristically
chauvinist
chief, chiefs
chimneys
chocolates
circuit
citizens
climbed
cocoa
coconut
collaborate
collapse
collapsible
colleague
college
collision
colloquial
colonel (in the army)
colossal
column
commemorate
commend
commerce
commission
commit
commitment
committed
committee
commotion
comparatively
comparison
compel(ling)
competent
competition
completely
complimentary (praising)

comprehensible
compulsory
concede
conceit
conceive
concentrate
condemn
conference
conjure
connoisseur
conqueror
conscience
conscientious
conscious
consensus
consistent
conspiracy
conspirator
constituency
contemporary
controlled
controversial
convertible
coolly
correspondence
corroborate
corrupt
counterfeit
courageous
courteous
courtesy
crescendo(s)
critically
criticism
cruelly
curiosity

curious
cynically
cynicism

dairy, dairies (for milk)
debt
debtor
deceit
decision
deferring
definite(ly)
degradation
delicacy
delicately
democracy
derelict
descendant
describe
description
desiccated
despair
desperately
despicable
detached
deteriorate
deterrent
devastate
develop(ed)
development
diamond
diarrhea
diary, diaries (book)
die, died, dying
diesel
difference
digital

dilapidated
dilemma
dilettante
dimensions
disability
disagreement
disappear(ance)
disappoint(ment)
disapprove
disastrous
disciple
disciplinary
discotheque
disguise
disillusioned
disintegrate
disobedience
dissatisfied
disservice
dissimilar
dissolve
dissuade
doubtful(ly)
drastically
drunkenness
duly
dungeon
dutiful

earnest
easily
eccentric
echo, echoes
ecstasy
eerie
eerily

effervescence
efficiency
eight(h)
eighteen
eighty
either
elegant
eloquence
embarrass(ment)
embellish
emergency
emotion
emperor
empress
emptiness
encyclopedia
endeavor
enormous
environment
equality
equatorial
equipped
especially
eventual(ly)
exaggerate
exceed
excessive
excel(ling)
excellent
exceptional(ly)
excitement
exciting
exclaim
exclamation
exercise
exhaust

exhibition
exhilarating
existence
expense
experience
extension
extraordinary
extravagant
extremely
exuberant

facilities
factories
Fahrenheit
failure
faithful(ly)
fallacy
familiar
family, families
famous
fantasies
fantastically
fascination
fastening
fatiguing
favorable
favorite
feasible
February
feign (pretend)
feminine
ferociously
fictitious
fidgeted
field
fierce(ly)

fiery
fifth
finally
finish
fluorescent
forbidden
foreboding (foretelling)
forecast
foreign
forfeit
forgivable
fortieth
forty
fourteen
fragrance
frantically
freight (cargo)
friend
fulfilled
fully
furniture
further
future

gaiety
gaily
galloped
gardener
gardening
gas, gases
general(ly)
generosity
generous
ghetto
ghost
giraffe

glimpse
glorious
goddess
gorgeous
gorilla (ape)
gossiped
government
governor
gracious
gradual(ly)
graffiti (plural)
grammar
grammatical
granary
grandeur
grateful(ly)
gratitude
greasy
grief
grievance
grievous
gruesome
guarantee
guaranteed
guard
guardian
guerrilla (raiding soldier)
guest
guidance
guide
guilty
guise (manner)

half, halves
handicapped
handkerchief(s) (*or* -ves)

happened
happily
happiness
harass(ment)
hassle
hastened
hazard
heaven
height
heir(ess)
hemorrhage
hero, heroes
hideous
hindrance
historically
holiday
honestly
hoofs *or* hooves
horror
horrified
horrifying
Hungary
hungrily
hungry
hygiene
hymn
hypocrisy
hypocrite
hypocritically
hysterical (in a frenzy)

icicle
identical(ly)
idiosyncrasy
idyllic
illegal(ly)

illegible
illiterate
imaginary
imitate
immature
immediate(ly)
immense(ly)
immoral
immortal
inadequate
in between (2 words)
incidentally
incredible
incurred
indebted
indefinite(ly)
independent
indestructible
indictment
    (criminal charge)
indispensable
in fact (2 words)
inferred
infinite(ly)
inflammable
information
innate
innocent
innuendo(es)
innumerable
inoculate
inspired
in spite of (3 words)
installation
insurrection
intellectual

intelligible
intention(ally)
interested
interference
interpreted
interrupt
intimate(ly)
intriguing
introduce
invisible
involvement
iridescent
irrecoverable
irregular(ly)
irrelevant
irreparable
irreplaceable
irresistible
irresponsibly
irreverent
irreversible
irritably
irritate
island
isle (island)
itinerary

jealous
jeopardy
jockeys
journey, journeys
judgment (*or* judgement)
juicy
justifying
justified

keenness

khaki
knife, knives
knitting
knowledgeable
knuckles

laboratory
lady, ladies
laid (never layed)
language
latitude
leapt (*or* leaped)
legendary
leisure
length
leopard
liaison
librarian
library, libraries
lieutenant
likelihood
limited
listener
literary
literature
livelihood
loaf, loaves
loneliness
longitude
luxury
lying

magazine
magic
magnificent
maintain

maintenance
manageable
managing
maneuver
mantelpiece
margarine
marriage
married
marvelous
massacre
mattress
meanness
meant
measure
mechanically
medically
medicine
medieval *or* mediaeval
Mediterranean
melancholy
merriment
messenger
metaphor(s)
meteorology
mimic
mimicking
miniature
ministry, ministries
minuscule
minute (tiny and 60 secs)
miraculous
miscellaneous
mischief
mischievous
mislaid
misshapen

misspell
moccasin
momentarily
monastery
monkey, monkeys
mortgage
motto, mottoes
mountainous
moustache(s)
murmuring
mystery
mystifying

naïve
naturally
necessarily
necessary
necessity
negotiate
neighbors
neither
nephew
nickel
niece
ninety
ninth
noisily
noticeable
nuclear
nuisance

obedient
obituary
obscene
obstacle
occasional(ly)

occupied
occupying
occurred
offered
often
old-fashioned
omitted
omission
opened
operation
opinion
opportunity
opponent
opposition
ordinary
original(ly)
outfitters
outrageous
overall
overrule

paid (never payed)
pamphlet
panel
panic
panicked
panic-stricken
pantomime
paragraph
parallel
paralysis
paralyze
paraphernalia
parliament
particular(ly)
pastime

patience
patiently
pavilion
peaceful(ly)
peculiar(ly)
penicillin
perceive
perhaps
perilous
permanent
permitted
perseverance
persistent
perspiration
persuade
persuasion
pharmacist
phenomena (plural)
phenomenally
phenomenon (singular)
photos
phrase
physical(ly)
physique
pianos
picnic
picnicking
piercing
pigeon
pitch, pitches
pitiful
pitiless
playwright
pleasant
pneumonia
poisonous

pony, ponies
popular
Portuguese
possession
potato, potatoes
predator
predecessor
preference
preferred
prejudice
premier
preparation
presence
pretence
pretension
pretentious
prevail
prevalent
previous
priest
primarily
primeval
primitive
princess, princesses
privilege
probably
procedure
procession
proclamation
profess
professionally
professor
proficient
profited
pronunciation
proofs

propaganda
propeller
protein
protrude
prove
psalm
psychiatrist
psychologically
psychology
publicly
pulley, pulleys
punctuation
pursue
pursuit
pyramid

quality
quarrel
quarter
quay (wharf)
queue

rarely
rarity
realize
really
reassurance
recede
recession
receipt
receive
recipe, recipes
recognize
recommend
reconnaissance
reconnoiter

recurring
referee
reference
referring
regrettable
regularity
regularly
relevant
relief
relieved
religious
remembrance
reminiscence
Renaissance
renowned
repel
repellent
repetition
resemble
resemblance
reservoir
resistance
responsibility
restaurant
retrieve
rheumatism
rhinoceros
rhyme
rhythm
ridicule
ridiculous
roof, roofs
routine

sacrilegious
safely

safety
said (past of *say*)
sandal
satellite
Saturday
scandal
scarcely
scarcity
scene
scenery
schedule
scheme
scholar
scholastic
school
science
scientifically
scissors
scream
screech
secondary
secrecy
secretary
seize
sense
sentence
separate
separation
sergeant
series
serviceable
severely
sheikh *or* sheik
shelf, shelves
shepherd
sheriff

shield
shriek
shyer
siege
sieve
silhouette
similarity
similarly
simile, similes
simultaneous
sincere(ly)
sincerity
singeing (burning)
skein (of wool)
skiing
skillful *or* skilful
slanderous
slyness
soldier
solemn(ly)
solicit
solicitor
soliloquy, soliloquies
souvenirs
sovereignty
spacious
speak
speech
specially
species
specific
sphere
sponsor
spoonful(s)
sprightly
squalid

squalor
squawk
statistically
statistician
stomach
strength
stubbornness
subtle
subtlety
subtly
succeed
successful(ly)
successor
succumb
suddenness
suffering
suggestion
superintendent
supersede
supervise
supervisor
supposed
suppression
sure (certain)
surfeit
surprise
surround
surveyor
survivors
susceptible
suspense
syllabus
symmetrically
symmetry
sympathetically
sympathy

symphony

talent
tariff
tattoo(s)
technical(ly)
technicality
technique
temperature
temporarily
temporary
tenant
tendency
terrible
terrifically
terrify
theater (*or* theatre)
thief, thieves
thorough
threshold
tidiness
tobacco
tobogganing
tomato, tomatoes
tomorrow (1 word)
tongue
torpedo, torpedoes
tractor
traffic
trafficking
tragedy
tragically
transferred
transmitted
treachery
truly

truthfully
tried
trying
Tuesday
twelfth
tying (a knot)
typical(ly)
tyranny

ultimately
uncontrollable
unconscious
underrate
undoubtedly
universities
unnamed
unnatural
unnecessary
unnoticed
unsuccessful
until
usually

vaccinate
vacuum
valley(s)
valuable
variety
various
vegetable
vehicle
veil
vendor
vengeance

vertical(ly)
veterinary
veto, vetoes
vicious (cruel)
view
vigorous
vilify
villain
visible
visited
visitor
volcano, volcanoes
volley(s)
volunteered
voluntarily
voluntary

warily
weariness
Wednesday
weigh
weight
weird
welcome
welfare
whereas (1 word)
whisper
whistle
whole
wholly
wife, wives
wintry
wiry
wisdom

wisely

wisp

witch, witches

withhold

witticism

wittily

wreak (vengeance)

wrecked

wrench

writhing

yacht

yield

## SOME HELPFUL RULES

### 1 *i* before *e* except after *c*, if the sound is *ee*

e.g. believe, achieve, chief, siege, deceit, receipt, ceiling

(Exceptions to the rule: either, neither, sheik, leisure, caffeine, seize, counterfeit, weir(d), protein, plebeian, species, financier.)

**Note:** When the sound is not pronounced *ee*, the spelling is *ei*.

e.g. neighbor, height, weight, foreign, their

(There are only four exceptions to this: friend, sieve, mischief, and handkerchief.)

## 2 **Verbs ending in** *-ceed* **and** *-cede*

With *suc-, ex-,* and *pro-*
Double *ee* must go.

Only three words end in *-ceed:* succeed, exceed, proceed.

Otherwise: intercede, precede, recede, concede.

## 3 *c* or *s*?

Usually the noun has *c;* the verb *s.*

e.g. prophecy (noun) to prophesy (verb)
advice (noun)   to advise (verb)

(In some cases either *c* or *s* is used for both the noun and the verb, e.g., practice, license.)

## 4 **Doubling the letter before** *-ing, -ed* (and other suffixes that start with a vowel, e.g., *-er, -est, -able*)

The final consonant is doubled before *-ing, -ed,* etc.

**(a)** in words of one syllable ending in a single vowel followed by a single consonant (e.g., tap, hop):

Distinguish: shinning (up a tree), shining (sun)
starring, staring; scarred, scared
dinning (it into you), dining (room)
dinner, diner (A diner eats a dinner.)

**(b)** in longer words ending in a single vowel followed by a single consonant, where the stress falls on the *last* syllable.

e.g. begin(ning), occur(red), (p)referred, committed, admitted, fulfilling, regrettable, forgettable

but *not* when the stress is elsewhere:

e.g. offer(ing), happening, benefited, galloped, preference

(Exceptions: handicapped, kidnapped.)


## 5  Plurals

The general rule is to add an *"s,"* or, after *s, x, ch, sh, z,* to add *"es."*

**(a)** If the noun ends in a consonant followed by a *y,* drop the *y* and add *ies:*

e.g. fairy — fairies; monastery — monasteries
     lady — ladies; ally — allies; story — stories

If the noun ends in a vowel followed by *y,* simply add *s:*

e.g. donkeys, valleys, monkeys, chimneys, alleys, boys, trays

**(b)** Nouns ending in *i,* add *s:*

e.g. alibis, rabbis

**(c)** Nouns ending in *o,* EXCEPT for those listed below, add *s:*

e.g. pianos, dynamos, photos

(Exceptions: tomatoes, potatoes, heroes, mosquitoes, echoes, mottoes, torpedoes, cargoes, volcanoes, vetoes, embargoes, tornadoes, dominoes, buffaloes, desperadoes, haloes, noes.)

**(d)** Nouns ending in *f* and *fe.* There is no rule, though attention to the pronunciation helps:

e.g. calves, wives, knives, halves, shelves, thieves, loaves, roofs, proofs, chiefs

Some have either:

e.g. hoofs/hooves, wharfs/wharves

**(e)** Some nouns keep their foreign plurals:

e.g. crisis — crises; oasis — oases
criterion — criteria; phenomenon — phenomena
terminus — termini (or -uses); larva — larvae
medium — media (but mediums to contact ghosts)

**(f)** Hyphenated compounds usually add the *s* to the main noun part:

e.g. passers-by, sons-in-law

**(g)** Some nouns have the same form in singular and plural:

e.g. sheep, aircraft, moose, deer, fish, flour, coffee, swine

**(h)** For some nouns, the difference between the singular and the plural form is in their vowels:

e.g. foot/feet, goose/geese, louse/lice, man/men, mouse/mice, tooth/teeth

# 6 Word with prefix *dis-* or *mis-*

Do not add extra letters when a word contains the prefix *dis-* or *mis-:*

e.g. dis + appear = disappear
     dis + appoint = disappoint

A double *s* will appear only when the word to which the prefix is added starts with an *s:*

e.g. service     disservice
     spell        misspell
     satisfied   dissatisfied

# 7 Suffixes *-ful, -fully; -al, -ally*

**(a)** Adjectives formed with the suffix *-ful* or *-al* (e.g., careful, actual) have one *l*.

**(b)** When forming adverbs add *-ly* as usual:

e.g. careful      carefully
     beautiful   beautifully
     real         really
     accidental  accidentally
     actual       actually

**(c)** Adjectives ending in *-ic* form adverbs by adding *-ically* (except *publicly*):

e.g. basically, terrifically, fantastically

## 8   Words ending in a silent *e*

**(a)** These usually keep the *e* before suffixes that begin with a consonant:

e.g. hopeful, arrangement, sincerely, completely

(Exceptions: argument, truly, duly, wholly.)

**(b)** If the suffix begins with a vowel, the *e* is usually dropped:

e.g. come — coming; argue — arguing;
     inquire — inquiry; subtle — subtly

(Verbs ending in *-oe* do not drop the *e:*

e.g. canoeing, hoeing.)

**(c)** After words ending in *-ce* or *-ge* the *e* must be kept so that the *c/g* remains a "soft" sound (i.e., as in Cecil or George, not "hard" as in catgut):

e.g. noticeable, serviceable, manageable, courageous, singeing (burning)

(Contrast the pronunciation of singing, navigable, practicable.)

## 9 Words ending in -*y*

**(a)** Words ending in -*y* preceded by a consonant change the *y* to *i* before any suffix except -*ing*:

e.g.
| | | |
|---|---|---|
| cry | cried | crying |
| try | tries | trying |
| dry | dries, drier | drying |
| satisfy | satisfied | satisfying |
| hungry | hungrier, hungrily | |
| necessary | necessarily | |

(Exceptions: shyly, slyer, spryest, dryness.)

**(b)** Verbs like *lie, die, tie* become *lying, dying, tying*. (To *dye* [clothes] becomes *dyeing*.)

## 10 Words ending in *c*

These add a *k* to keep the *c* hard when adding suffixes beginning with *e, i,* or *y:*

e.g.
| | |
|---|---|
| picnic | picnicking |
| mimic | mimicked |
| traffic | trafficker |
| colic | colicky |
| panic | panicky |

## 11 Prefixes *fore-, for-; ante-, anti-*

**(a)** The prefix *fore-* means in front or beforehand:

e.g. forewarn, forecast, forestall, foreground

(Contrast: forbid, forbearance.)

**(b)** *Ante-* means before; *anti-* means against:

e.g. antenatal, anteroom; antidote, antiseptic

## 12  "Joins" within words

Do not add or subtract letters at the "joins" within words:

e.g. keenness, unnecessary, overrule, interrupt, drunkenness, withhold

# 2 Words often confused

(See also **Common faults,** subsection 10, p. 63)

| | |
|---|---|
| **accept** | to receive |
| **except** | to omit, exclude; not including |
| **adapt** | to adjust |
| **adopt** | to accept and approve, take as one's own |
| **affect** (verb) | to influence or produce an effect on |
| **effect** (noun or verb) | a result; to bring about or accomplish |
| **aggravate** | to make worse |
| **irritate** | to annoy, exasperate |
| **air** | the mixture of gases that surrounds the earth |
| **heir** | one who inherits, a beneficiary |
| **alibi** | a fact or claim that one was elsewhere |
| **excuse** | an apology offered |

| | |
|---|---|
| **allowed** | permitted |
| **aloud** | audibly, loudly |
| **allusion** (to) | a casual or indirect reference |
| **illusion** | a false impression or image; a magician's trick |
| **delusion** | a deception, mistaken belief |
| **already** | by this time |
| **all ready** | all persons (things) are ready |
| **altogether** | completely |
| **all together** | all in one place |
| **altar** | a place for worship |
| **alter** | to change |
| **always** | ever, constantly |
| **all ways** | all directions or methods |
| **amount** | How much? (weight or money) |
| **number** | How many? (individual items) |
| **ascent** | an upward climb |
| **assent** | to agree, agreement |
| **astrology** | foretelling the future by the stars |
| **astronomy** | science of the planets and stars |
| **bail** | security for a court appearance |
| **bale** | a bundle |
| **bare** | naked; to uncover |
| **bear** | to carry; an animal |
| **base** | a basis, support |
| **bass** | a low deep tone; a fish |
| **beach** | a shore |
| **beech** | a tree |

| | |
|---|---|
| **berth** | a sleeping place, a bunk |
| **birth** | the act of being born |
| **beside** | at the side of |
| **besides** | in addition to |
| **bloc** | a group of nations acting as a unit |
| **block** | a piece of material; an obstacle |
| **board** | a plank, table; to receive meals; to go on board |
| **bored** | weary with tediousness; made a hole |
| **boarder** | a lodger (with meals) |
| **border** | edge, limit |
| **born** | to come into the world by birth |
| **borne** | carried, endured |
| **borough** | an incorporated town |
| **burro** | a donkey |
| **burrow** | a hole in which an animal lives; (to) excavate |
| **brake** | to put the brakes on (e.g., a car) |
| **break** | to shatter; an interval |
| **breath** | air drawn into lungs |
| **breathe** | to draw air into lungs |
| **bridal** | nuptial, pertaining to a wedding |
| **bridle** | a device to control a horse; to curb, restrain |
| **Britain** | the country |
| **Briton** | the inhabitant |
| **broach** | to open (e.g., a subject for discussion) |
| **brooch** | an ornament |

| | |
|---|---|
| **cannon** | a gun |
| **canon** | a churchman; church law |
| **canvas** | coarse cloth for tent, etc. |
| **canvass** | to solicit votes, orders, etc. |
| **capital** | chief; punishable by death; the chief city of a state or country; a sum of money |
| **capitol** | the building in which the legislature meets |
| **carat** | a measure of the weight of a precious stone |
| **caret** | a proofreader's mark to indicate an insertion |
| **carrot** | a vegetable |
| **karat** | a measure of the purity of gold |
| **cede** | to yield, surrender |
| **seed** | a spore, egg, sperm |
| **cereal** | a breakfast food |
| **serial** | in a sequence; a story told in parts |
| **ceremonial** | of a ritual or ceremony, formal |
| **ceremonious** | too much concerned with formalities, showy |
| **choose** | present tense of *to choose* |
| **chose** | past tense of *to choose* |
| **cite** | mention, refer to |
| **sight** | vision; something that is seen |
| **site** | position, location |
| **civic** | of a city |
| **civil** | polite; not military (e.g., "Civil Service") |

| | |
|---|---|
| **climactic** | of a climax |
| **climatic** | of climate |
| **clothes** | garments |
| **cloths** | pieces of cloth |
| **coarse** | rough, harsh, crude |
| **course** | path, route (e.g., for racing, golf); the division of a meal; a series; "of course" |
| **compare** | to point out similarities |
| **contrast** | to point out differences |
| **complement** | that which makes up or completes |
| **compliment** | praise |
| **contemporary** | existing at the same time as |
| **modern** | up-to-date |
| **contemptible** | vile, mean |
| **contemptuous** | showing or feeling scorn |
| **continual** | frequent, repeated (e.g., dripping tap) |
| **continuous** | connected, unbroken (e.g., stream of water) |
| **core** | the hard center of fruit |
| **corps** | a unit of soldiers or other persons |
| **council** | an assembly |
| **counsel** | advice; legal adviser; to advise |
| **credible** | believable |
| **creditable** | deserving praise |
| **credulous** | inclined to believe; gullible |

| | |
|---|---|
| **currant** | small berry |
| **current** | now running, in general use; flow of water, electricity, air |
| **decease** | death |
| **disease** | illness |
| **defective** | faulty |
| **deficient** | lacking |
| **defer** | postpone |
| **differ** | be unlike |
| **definite** | fixed, certain, clear |
| **definitive** | final, complete, thorough |
| **deprecate** | to express disapproval of |
| **depreciate** | to go down in value, rate less highly |
| **desert** | barren place; that which is deserved; to abandon |
| **dessert** | sweet course in a meal |
| **detract** (from) | to lessen, take away from |
| **distract** | to divert (attention) |
| **diner** | one who eats; a restaurant |
| **dinner** | a meal |
| **disburse** | to pay out money |
| **disperse** | to scatter, spread (or vanish) |
| **discover** | to find something which was always there |
| **invent** | to create or devise something new |
| **discreet** | prudent, wary |
| **discrete** | separate, unconnected |

| | |
|---|---|
| **disinterested** | neutral, unbiased |
| **uninterested** | lacking interest, not interested |
| **dose** | quantity of medicine to be taken at one time |
| **doze** | to sleep |
| **dual** | double, composed of two |
| **duel** | a fight between two people |
| **dyeing** | coloring |
| **dying** | almost dead |
| **economic** | of finances |
| **economical** | being careful, thrifty |
| **effective** | having an effect; coming into operation |
| **effectual** | answering its purpose |
| **efficacious** | sure to produce the desired effect |
| **efficient** | competent; working productively |
| **elicit** | to draw out |
| **illicit** | not legal |
| **eligible** | fit to be chosen |
| **illegible** | indecipherable |
| **emigrant** | one who leaves the country |
| **immigrant** | one who enters the country |
| **eminent** | prominent, distinguished |
| **imminent** | threatening near at hand |
| **envelop** | to surround or cover |
| **envelope** | a flat wrapper for a letter or a thin package |
| **especially** | notably, particularly |
| **specially** | for a special occasion or purpose |

| | |
|---|---|
| **exceptionable** | objectionable |
| **exceptional** | unusual |
| **fact** | a truth, actual happening |
| **factor** | a contributory element, cause |
| **faint** | to swoon; dim, indistinct, weak |
| **feint** | sham attack or blow; to pretend to do something |
| **fatal** | resulting in death |
| **fateful** | deciding one's fate |
| **flaunt** | to show off |
| **flout** | to treat with scorn |
| **flea** | an insect |
| **flee** | to run away |
| **flew** | past tense of *fly;* to soar |
| **flu** | influenza |
| **flue** | chimney, smokestack |
| **flowed** | past participle of *to flow* (water) |
| **flown** | past participle of *to fly* (birds) |
| **foregoing** | preceding, gone before |
| **forgoing** | giving up, abstaining from |
| **formally** | in a formal manner |
| **formerly** | previously |
| **fortuitous** | happening by chance |
| **fortunate** | having or bringing good luck |
| **foul** | dirty, bad-smelling |
| **fowl** | a bird |
| **gait** | a manner of walking, e.g., sauntering |
| **gate** | a means of entering or leaving |

| | |
|---|---|
| **genteel** | affectedly elegant |
| **gentle** | not rough |
| **guerilla** | raiding soldier |
| **gorilla** | ape |
| **hanged** | executed ("hanged by the neck") |
| **hung** | other uses of the verb *to hang* |
| **heal** | to mend |
| **heel** | part of the foot |
| **hear** | to perceive sound, listen to |
| **here** | at this place |
| **hoard** | a hidden stockpile |
| **horde** | a crowd, multitude |
| **human** | of man as opposed to animal or god |
| **humane** | compassionate, kind |
| **idle** | unoccupied, unemployed |
| **idol** | an object of worship; a dearly beloved or admired person |
| **idyll (idyl)** | a pastoral or romantic work |
| **illegible** | indecipherable |
| **ineligible** | not fit to be chosen |
| **imaginary** | of a thing that exists only in the imagination |
| **imaginative** | having a high degree of imagination |
| **imperial** | of an empire or emperor |
| **imperious** | proud, domineering |
| **imply** | to hint (speaker implies) |
| **infer** | to draw a conclusion (hearer infers) |

| | |
|---|---|
| **impracticable** | that cannot be put into effect |
| **impractical** | not having practical skill; not suited to actual conditions |
| **industrial** | of industry |
| **industrious** | hardworking |
| **ingenious** | skillful in inventing |
| **ingenuous** | artless, innocent |
| **intellectual** | of the mind, having superior powers of reasoning; a person who is concerned with things of the mind (as opposed to feelings) |
| **intelligent** | clever |
| **intelligible** | clear, understandable |
| **into** | entering, inside (e.g., He went into the house.) |
| **in to** | (separate senses) (e.g., She came in to tell us the news.) |
| **it's** | it is (or it has) |
| **its** | belonging to it |
| **judicial** | connected with a judge or law court |
| **judicious** | having sound judgment |
| **larva** | caterpillar, etc. |
| **lava** | from a volcano |
| **lead** | metal; present tense of *to lead* |
| **led** | past tense of *to lead* |
| **less** | smaller in amount |
| **fewer** | smaller in number |
| **lightening** | making less heavy or less dark |
| **lightning** | a flash of |

| | |
|---|---|
| **liqueur** | strong sweet drink |
| **liquor** | any alcoholic drink |
| **loath/loth** | reluctant, unwilling |
| **loathe** | to dislike greatly |
| **loose** | to unfasten; not tight |
| **lose** | to fail to win; fail to keep |
| **luxuriant** | growing profusely |
| **luxurious** | very comfortable; self-indulgent |
| **marshal** | officer; to arrange in due order |
| **martial** | of war or the army (court-martialled) |
| **masterful** | imperious, domineering |
| **masterly** | expert, skillful |
| **maybe** | perhaps |
| **may be** | e.g., it may be . . . |
| **momentary** | short-lived |
| **momentous** | important |
| **moral** | right, virtuous; a lesson from a story |
| **morale** | mental state of confidence |
| **negligent** | careless |
| **negligible** | small or unimportant |
| **new** | opposite of old |
| **knew** | past tense of *to know* |
| **notable** | worth noting |
| **noticeable** | easy to see, prominent |
| **observance** | obeying, paying heed to (a rule or custom) |
| **observation** | noting, looking at |

| | |
|---|---|
| **official** | connected with an office; authorized |
| **officious** | meddlesome |
| **oral** | spoken (of the mouth) |
| **aural** | pertaining to the ear |
| **verbal** | in words (spoken or written) |
| **palate** | the roof of the mouth |
| **palette** | an artist's board for mixing colors |
| **pallet** | a cot, bunk, berth |
| **partake of** | to take or share (food or rest) |
| **participate in** | to take part in |
| **passed** | past tense of *to pass;* went by |
| **past** | a former time; beyond |
| **peace** | opposite of war; quiet |
| **piece** | a portion or part |
| **pedal** | a foot lever |
| **peddle** | to sell |
| **persecute** | to oppress, harass |
| **prosecute** | to take legal proceedings against |
| **personal** | individual, private |
| **personnel** | employees or staff |
| **plain** | flat country; clear; undecorated; unattractive |
| **plane** | level surface; to shave level; tool; tree; airplane |
| **pray** | to worship, beg |
| **prey** | hunted animal; plunder |
| **precede** | to go before in arrangement or rank |
| **proceed** | to go along, continue |

| | |
|---|---|
| **precedence** | the act or fact of preceding; priority |
| **precedents** | examples, models, standards |
| **precipitate** | hasty, rash |
| **precipitous** | steep |
| **prescribe** | to order, lay down as a rule |
| **proscribe** | to condemn; prohibit |
| **principal** | chief, most important |
| **principle** | truth, law, idea; code of conduct |
| **profit** | financial gain |
| **prophet** | religious forecaster |
| **quiet** | silent |
| **quite** | fairly, very, completely |
| **rain** | water from the clouds; to fall as water |
| **reign** | to rule |
| **rein** | to check, restrain |
| **raise(d)** | to lift, make grow, increase |
| **raze (rase)** | to demolish, level to the ground |
| **rise (rose)** | to get up or go up |
| **recourse** | "to have recourse to" (to resort to) |
| **resource** | source of supply; device; ingenuity |
| **re-cover** | to cover again |
| **recover** | to regain health, regain possession of |
| **reek** | to smell strongly, to give an impression |
| **wreak** | to inflict damage |

| | |
|---|---|
| **re-form**<br>**reform** | to form again<br>to correct, improve |
| **re-sign**<br>**resign** | to sign again<br>to give up (e.g., a job or office) |
| **respectable**<br>**respectful**<br>**respective** | worthy of respect<br>showing respect<br>relating to each in order |
| **review**<br>**revue** | survey, inspection<br>a stage production |
| **right**<br><br>**rite**<br>**wright**<br>**write** | opposite of left or wrong; just claim or due<br>ceremony (religious)<br>a workman (e.g., playwright)<br>to put words on paper |
| **rogue**<br>**rouge** | a villain<br>a cosmetic for coloring the cheeks red |
| **rout**<br>**route** | a defeat<br>a course, way, or road for passage or travel; to direct |
| **scarce**<br><br>**rare** | of ordinary things temporarily not plentiful<br>of things infrequent at all times |
| **seasonable**<br>**seasonal** | suitable to the occasion or season<br>occurring at a particular season |
| **sensible**<br>**sensitive** | showing good sense<br>capable of feeling deeply; responsive to slight changes |
| **sensual**<br>**sensuous** | indulging the senses<br>relating to the senses |

| | |
|---|---|
| **sew** | i.e., with a needle |
| **sow** | i.e., with seeds |
| **shear** | to shave, cut |
| **sheer** | steep; absolute; transparent; to swerve |
| **sight** | thing seen; faculty of vision |
| **site** | location, position, plot |
| **soar** | to fly high |
| **sore** | painful |
| **sociable** | enjoying company |
| **social** | pertaining to society |
| **solidarity** | show of support for, holding the same interest as |
| **solidity** | state of being firm, stable, or solid |
| **staid** | sedate, sober |
| **stayed** | past tense of *stay;* remained |
| **stalactite** | comes down from "ceiling" of a cave |
| **stalagmite** | grows up from the ground |
| **stationary** | not moving |
| **stationery** | writing materials |
| **stimulant** | alcohol, drug |
| **stimulus** | incentive |
| **straight** | not bent, direct |
| **strait(s)** | narrow places, difficulties |
| **suit** | fit; set of clothes or cards |
| **suite** | a number of things forming a series or set (e.g., rooms, furniture) |

| | |
|---|---|
| **superficial** | on the surface, shallow |
| **superfluous** | too many, more than is needed |
| **taught** | past tense of *to teach* |
| **taut** | tight, tense |
| **temporal** | earthly (as opposed to spiritual or eternal) |
| **temporary** | not permanent |
| **their** | belonging to them |
| **there** | in that place; "there is" |
| **they're** | they are |
| **threw** | past tense of *to throw* |
| **through** | from one end or side to the other; by means of |
| **thorough** | complete, in detail; very careful |
| **to** | always used except for: |
| **too** | also or in an excessive degree ("too hot") |
| **two** | number |
| **translucent** | allowing light through but not transparent |
| **transparent** | that can be seen through |
| **urban** | of a town |
| **urbane** | well-bred, suave, civilized |
| **vain** | conceited |
| **vane** | a wind indicator, weathercock |
| **vein** | a blood vessel |
| **vial** | a small bottle |
| **vile** | disgusting, morally repulsive |
| **vice** | evil, wickedness |
| **vise** | a tool for holding |

| | |
|---|---|
| **vicious** | cruel |
| **viscous** | thick and gluey |
| **waist** | a part of the body |
| **waste** | rubbish, barren land |
| **waive** | to set aside, forgo (a claim, right, rule) |
| **wave** | shake or move to and fro; curve(s) of water, hair, sound, heat, etc. |
| **weather** | sunshine, wind, rain, etc. |
| **whether** | if |
| **were** | past tense of *to be* |
| **we're** | we are |
| **where** | in what place? |
| **who's** | who is (or has) |
| **whose** | belonging to whom |
| **yoke** | a bar or frame to join two work animals |
| **yolk** | the yellow part of an egg |
| **your** | belonging to you |
| **you're** | you are |

# 3 Punctuation

(See also **Useful terms**, p. 90)

## 1 The period

**(a)** marks the end of a sentence (except for questions and exclamations). A sentence is a complete unit of sense that can stand on its own. (It may consist of only one word as in greetings like "Hello.", commands like "Stop." [where the subject — *you* — is understood], and replies like "No.".)

To test whether a group of words is a sentence, you should read it aloud to yourself; if it conveys a complete meaning, then you can probably put a period at the end.

**(b)** indicates an abbreviation.

e.g. Co.   etc.   i.e.   a.m.

## 2 Capital letters are used

**(a)** at the beginning of every sentence.

**(b)** at the beginning of a passage of direct quotation (see subsection 6 below).

**(c)** for proper nouns (i.e., names of *particular* persons, places, things), and for months of the year and days of the week:

e.g. Jane, Everest, Liverpool, July, Monday

**(d)** for adjectives derived from proper nouns, especially places and people:

e.g. English, French, Victorian, Elizabethan

(except for common compounds like brussels sprouts and venetian blinds, where the adjective has lost its original emphasis).

**(e)** for the first and all main words in *any kind of title:*
  books, plays, poems (e.g., *Far from the Madding Crowd*)
  films, T.V. programs (e.g., *Masterpiece Theater*)
  newspapers and magazines (e.g., *Time*)
  names of ships, houses, inns
  a person's title (e.g., Governor of New York)
  the titles of institutions and businesses (e.g., Women's Institute)

**(f)** at the beginning of each line of verse (except in some modern poetry).

**(g)** for the pronoun *I*.

**(h)** when a noun is personified or considered as a grand abstract idea:

e.g. "The Child is Father of the Man."

**(i)** for *He, His,* when referring to God.

## 3   The question mark

This is used for all direct questions:

e.g. What are you doing?
     You will come, won't you?

but *not* for reported questions:

e.g. I wonder what he is doing.
     Ask him who did it.

(Don't forget the question mark at the end of a long question.)

## 4   The exclamation mark

This expresses some kind of astonishment or a sharp outburst or comment:

e.g. Fire! Fire!

It can also add a tone of humor or sarcasm:

e.g. And he was supposed to be an expert!

(Don't overuse it and don't use more than one at a time.)

## 5   Commas

The following rules cover the main uses. (You will find that there are many other optional uses that lend emphasis or give a finer point of meaning.)

Commas are used

**(a)** to separate words, phrases or clauses in a list:

**(i)** a series of nouns:

e.g. His room was littered with books, pens, papers, and maps.

**(ii)** a series of adjectives:

e.g. He was a quiet, gentle, unassuming man.

When one adjective describes the other or when the last adjective is closely linked with its noun, there should be no comma:

e.g. the deep blue sky; a new state college

(Contrast: a thin, white hand)

**(iii)** a series of adverbs:

e.g. Try to work quickly, confidently, and efficiently.

**(iv)** a series of phrases:

e.g. We spent an enjoyable day visiting the zoo, rowing on the lake, and picnicking in the park.

**(v)** a series of verbs or clauses:

> e.g. He took a long run-up, slipped on the wet grass, and landed short of the sand-pit.

> (It is better with larger groupings to put a comma before the *and*.)

The comma is also used between two long main clauses joined by *and* or *but,* especially when the subjects of the clauses are different.

**(b)** before and after a phrase or clause in apposition (i.e., when placing a group of words after a noun to give a fuller explanation or description of it):

e.g. Jean, *Bill's elder sister,* brought home a new hat, *a pink one with feathers.*

**(c)** to separate "sentence adverbs" — these show the link between the whole sentence and the preceding one(s):

e.g. however, on the other hand, moreover
They tried hard. The conditions, *however,* were against them.

**(d)** to mark off the person(s) addressed or called to (whether by name or other description):

e.g. Look out, *Fred!* Now, *you fool,* you've missed it!

**(e)** to bracket off insertions or afterthoughts. (Dashes or parentheses may also be used for this.)

Use commas on either side of the parenthetical expression:

e.g. Sunday, *as everyone knows,* is a day of rest.

**(f)** to mark off interjections — words like *yes, no, please:*

e.g. *Well, er, no,* I don't think I will, *thank you.*

**(g)** before "tagging on" clauses like *don't you?* or *isn't it?:*

e.g. They played well, *didn't they?*

**(h)** to mark off a participial phrase:

e.g. *Seeing the lion,* Caesar screamed.

**(i)** to mark off adverbial clauses, especially when they start the sentence, except when they are very short. (Adverbial clauses are introduced by words like *although, if, because.*):

e.g. *Although you may not realize it,* you need two commas in this sentence, *because it contains two adverbial clauses.*

**(j)** to mark off an adjective clause which merely comments but does not limit or define:

e.g. The boys, *who were fooling,* were punished. (*Without* commas this would mean that *only* the boys who were fooling were punished; *with* commas it means that *all* the boys were fooling and were punished. The commas act like brackets.)

**Note:** Don't put a comma between the subject and its verb:

**Wrong:** What he wrote, was illegible.
**Right:**  What he wrote was illegible.

# 6 Punctuating conversation/direct quotations

**(a)** Start a new paragraph *every* time the speaker changes.

**(b)** The words spoken and the accompanying punctuation are enclosed in quotation marks.

**Note:** The punctuation comes *inside* the quotation marks.

**(c)** Even though the words spoken would form a sentence on their own, they are followed by a comma (not a period) when the verb and its subject come *afterwards:*

e.g. "We are going away," they said.
*but* "Where are you going?" he asked.

**(d)** When the subject and verb start the sentence, they are followed by a comma, and the first word spoken has a capital letter:

e.g. They said, "We are going away."

**(e)** When the quotation is interrupted to insert the verb and its subject, one comma is needed when breaking off the speech and another immediately before continuing it. The next word within the quotation marks has a small letter, because it is continuing the quoted sentence:

e.g. "I am not," he stressed, "particularly happy about this."

Consider the following two sentences:

"I am going," he said. "Do not try to stop me."

## 7  Quotation marks are also used

**(a)** when quoting someone's words or from a book:

e.g. "To be, or not to be" begins a famous speech from *Hamlet*.

Take care, when quoting from a book/play/poem, that your own sentence leads naturally into the quotation.

**(b)** when using foreign words, jargon, specialist words or slang; or to show that a word is used sarcastically. (In print these might be italicized.)

## 8  The apostrophe is used

**(a)** to denote *possession* with nouns. The singular noun takes an apostrophe followed by an *s*. Plurals ending in *s* add an apostrophe after the final *s:*

e.g. a lady's hat, the ladies' hats (i.e., the hats of the ladies)
a week's holiday, six weeks' holiday

an ass's burden, Dickens's novels, Charles's sister

Jones's cap, the Joneses' house (i.e., the house of the Joneses)

Be careful with unusual plurals (like men, children, mice) which are treated as if they were singular:

e.g. men's coats, women's rights, children's toys (*never* write mens' or childrens')

For proper nouns ending in a sounded *e* and an *s* or in *s* vowel *s* (e.g., Euripides, Moses) add the apostrophe after the *s:*

e.g. Ulysses' adventures, Archimedes' principle, Jesus' mother

(Note also — for goodness' sake.)

In units involving two or more nouns or in a compound noun or phrase, put the apostrophe on the last word only:

e.g. William and Mary's reign, my father-in-law's house

(This does not apply if there is no joint possession: e.g., my brother's and my sister's birthdays.)

**Note:** The apostrophe is *not* used in these words: yours, hers, ours, theirs or its (when it means belonging to it). (Would you write *hi's* for his?) It is, however, used in *one's* (belonging to one and one is/ one has).

**(b)** to indicate a *contraction*. The apostrophe is placed where the letter(s) has(have) been omitted:

e.g. didn't, can't, they're (they are), you're, we're, I'd, I'll, it's (meaning it is or it has)

(But note: shan't, won't.)

**(c)** for the plural form of certain *letters* and *figures,* although this apostrophe is now often omitted:

e.g. the three R's, P's and Q's, in the '60's, if's and but's

## 9 Dashes and parentheses

Two dashes are used when breaking off a sentence to insert an afterthought or an explanatory comment or short list:

e.g. In August last year — I was with my family at the time — I had a serious accident.
Nothing — food, plates, cutlery, pans — could be left unattended.

A single dash may be used

**(a)** when breaking off a sentence for an abrupt change of thought or when "tagging on" another construction:

e.g. The following day we had better luck — but that is another story.

**(b)** to emphasize a repeated word:

e.g. The new regime imposed rigid laws — laws which the police found difficult to enforce.

**(c)** when bringing together a number of items:

e.g. Toothbrush, can opener, matches, soap pads — these are often forgotten by inexperienced campers.

**(d)** with a colon to introduce a long quotation or list, although this usage is now dying out (this is called a pointer: — ).

**(e)** to signify missing letters:

e.g. D--- it!

Parentheses (always two) are, like dashes, used for "asides" and for enclosing additional information:

e.g. Citrus fruits (oranges, lemons, limes) are rich in vitamin C.

(Parentheses, like dashes, often carry the meaning of "that is" [i.e.] or "namely.")

(If there is a parenthetical *phrase* at the end of a sentence, the period follows the parenthesis; if the parentheses enclose a *sentence,* the period comes inside.)

## 10 Hyphens (and unhyphenated words)

The tendency is for commonly used compounds, especially those formed with a prefix, to be single, unhyphenated words, e.g., antiwar, midterm, multi-story, prerecorded, reexamined.

The hyphen is, however, used in the following cases:

**(a)** when the prefix is followed by a proper name:

e.g. mid-Atlantic, pre-Raphaelite, un-American

**(b)** when the prefix is stressed and might be confused with a twin compound:

e.g. re-sign, re-cover, re-form, un-ionized (contrast resign, recover, reform, unionized)

**(c)** when the compound forms an adjective *followed by* a noun, especially when confusion would result:

e.g. fifty-odd people (contrast fifty odd people), an ill-educated man, a fast-moving car, an out-of-work mechanic, a poverty-stricken family

**(d)** when the compound is formed from a phrase, especially one containing a preposition:

e.g. mother-in-law, bumper-to-bumper, devil-may-care attitude

**(e)** for compound numbers between 21 and 99 (e.g., sixty-four) to denote "up to and including" in numbers and dates (e.g., 1980-1990), and for fractions used as adjectives (e.g., a two-thirds majority).

(The hyphen also occurs in some compounds when the end of the first part of the compound has the same letter as the beginning of the next part, e.g., co-op, short-term.)

## 11  The semicolon is, or may be, used

**(a)** to separate clauses that could stand as sentences but which are *closely related*, especially

   **(i)** when the second clause *expands* or explains the first:

   e.g. Neither of us spoke; we merely waited in silence to see what would happen.

   **(ii)** when the clauses describe a *sequence* of actions or *different aspects* of the same topic:

   e.g. There was a sharp, bracing air; the ground was dry; the sea was crisp and clear.

   **(iii)** before independent clauses beginning with *even so, so, therefore, for instance, nevertheless, then*, etc.:

   e.g. He took great care; even so, he made a few errors.

   **(iv)** to suggest a contrast:

   e.g. I like swimming; my sister hates it.

(In all the above examples periods could have been used but would have been too abrupt.)

Note that the clause after the semicolon always begins with a small letter.

**(b)** to mark off a series of phrases (or clauses) which themselves contain commas:

e.g. You will need the following: some scrap paper; a pen, preferably blue or black; some envelopes; and some good, white, unlined writing paper.

## 12   The colon is used

**(a)** to introduce a list (e.g., as in 11(b) above), long quotation, or speech:

e.g. Speaking at Caesar's funeral, Antony addresses the crowd: "Friends, Romans, countrymen..."

It may also be used

**(b)** before a clause that explains (often by illustration) the previous statement. The colon has the force of the word "namely" or "that is":

e.g. One thing is certain: we shall not surrender. (Here a dash could have been used.)

**(c)** to express a *strong* contrast:

e.g. God creates: man destroys.

**(d)** to introduce a climax or concuding clause:

e.g. After pondering the choices before him, he came to a decision: he joined the army.

**(e)** to make a pointed connection:

e.g. Lenore became a director in just three months: her mother was the chief shareholder.

# 4 Common faults

(See also **Useful terms,** p. 90)

In a language which is constantly changing there is always some conflict between current usage and established practice. Similarly, there are differences between what is permissible in popular speech and what is expected in formal writing. The following constructions refer to usage in formal writing.

## 1  Agreement

A singular subject must have a singular verb-form, a plural subject a plural verb-form. Be sure to ask yourself whether the subject is singular or plural.

e.g. *One* of the men *was* guilty.
A *range* of goods *was* available.
All along the coast *lie traces* of oil slick.

**(a) Indefinite pronouns** — i.e., *anyone, someone, no one, none, (n)either* (when used without *(n)or*), *everyone, each* — are singular and should take a singular verb and be followed by *he, him, his,* and NOT *they, them, their(s):*

e.g. No one knows *his* own future.
     Anyone can do it if *he* tries *his* best.
     Each stood with *his* right hand behind *his* back.

**(b) (N)either ... (n)or.** If *both* the subjects are singular, the verb is also:

e.g. Neither the man nor the dog *was* in sight.

If one or both of the subjects are plural, the verb is plural:

e.g. Neither John nor his friends *are* coming.

**(c) This kind, this sort** (or **these kinds, these sorts**), but not "these kind," "these sort."

**(d) Collective nouns** (which are groups of persons or things) take a singular verb when considered as a complete unit:

e.g. The class *is* too large.

but a plural verb when considered as a number of separate persons or things:

e.g. The class *were* quarrelling.

**(e) The verb-form in an adjective clause** must agree with the right noun (or pronoun) in the clause before it:

e.g. She is one of the most famous writers who *have* ever lived.

     (*Who* relates back to *writers;* hence the plural *have*.)

## 2   Case

**(a) I, he, she, we, they,** and **who** are the subject.

e.g. The man who will be king . . .

**Wrong:** John and me are brothers.
**Right:** John and *I* are brothers.

**Wrong:** This is the man whom we all knew was guilty.
**Right:** This is the man *who* (we all knew) was guilty.
(The parentheses show that *who* is the subject of *was*.)
**or:** This is the man *whom* we all *knew to be* guilty.

**(b) Me, him, her, us, them** and **whom** are the object.

e.g. The man *whom* we met . . . (i.e., we met *him*.)

(*Whom* seems to be dying out of the language, but should be kept after prepositions:

e.g. To whom shall I send it?
. . . for whom the bell tolls.

but not when *who* is the subject of a noun clause:

e.g. There was some doubt about who did it.)

**Wrong:** Thank you for inviting Joan and I to dinner.
**Right:** Thank you for inviting Joan and *me* to dinner.

The objective case is used after all prepositions:

**Wrong:** He gave it to John and I.
**Right:** He gave it to John and *me*.

**Wrong:** between you and I; for you and he
**Right:** between you and *me;* for you and *him*

## 3  The confusing of pronouns, especially *one, you, it, he* and *they*

**(a)** If you start using the word *one* you must continue with it, though it can soon result in pomposity.

**Wrong:** One can easily spot your mistakes if you check carefully.
**Right:** One can easily spot one's mistakes if one checks carefully.
(Or, better still, use *you* and *your*.)

**(b)** Make sure, when using pronouns like *he, she, it* and *they,* that it is absolutely clear to whom or to what they refer.

**Wrong:** If the baby does not like fresh milk, boil it.
**Right:** Boil the milk if the baby does not like it fresh.

**Wrong:** As the bomb fell into the car, it stopped dead.
**Right:** The car stopped dead as the bomb fell into it.

**(c)** Do not confuse singular and plural.

**Wrong:**  The marigold is a fairly hardy plant; they grow in most soils.
**Right:**  Marigolds are fairly hardy plants; they grow in most soils.
  **or:**  The marigold is a fairly hardy plant; it grows in most soils.


## 4   The comparative and the superlative

The **comparative** applies to two:

e.g. He is the better player of the two.

The **superlative** applies to three or more:

e.g. He is the best swimmer in the county.

**Wrong:**  John is the tallest of the two brothers.
**Right:**  John is the *taller* of the two brothers.


## 5   The participial phrase

This is introduced by a verb-form ending in *-ing* or *-ed* and describes the noun (or pronoun) nearest to it, but outside the phrase itself. Such phrases are often wrongly related, or unattached.

**Wrong:**  Sitting on the veranda, the sun rose on our left. (This means that the sun was sitting on the veranda.)
**Right:**  Sitting on the veranda, *we* saw the sun rise on our left.

**Wrong:** Coming downstairs, the hall door opened.
(This means that the hall door was coming downstairs.)

**Right:** As he was coming downstairs, the hall door opened.

## 6  The gerund (or verbal noun)

This ends in *-ing* but acts as a *noun;* when qualified, it must, therefore, be preceded by an adjective (e.g., his, her, its, my, our, your, their):

**Wrong:** I don't like you leaving early.
**Right:** I don't like *your* leaving early. (It is the *leaving* I don't like.)

**Wrong:** I must escape without him knowing.
**Right:** I must escape without *his* knowing.

## 7  The subjunctive

This is rarely used now, but watch out for:

**(a)** Pure supposition: e.g., If I *were* king . . .

**(b)** After verbs of wishing: e.g., I wish she *were* here.

## 8  The position of common adverbs

(e.g., only, just, almost, even, mainly, also)

These should be placed immediately before the word they modify. Try inserting the word *only* in every possible position in this sentence:

> The bishop gave the baboon a bun.
> (Consider the different meanings.)

Care must also be taken with the placing of *both*, *(n)either . . . (n)or* and *not only . . . but also*.

**Wrong:** He not only plays tennis but also basketball.
**Right:** He plays not only tennis but also basketball.

(The two parts must be correctly balanced.)

## 9 The correct preposition

**(a)** different *from* (or *to*, not "than")

**(b)** to center *on*, *in* or *upon* (not "(a)round")

**(c)** to prefer this *to* that (not "than")

**(d)** anxious *about* (not "of")

**(e)** bored *with* or *by* (not "of")

**(f)** superior *to* (not "than")

**(g)** cover *with* (not "by")

## 10 Words commonly confused

**(a) Lie** and **lay**. *To lie* means to put yourself in a flat position; *to lay* means to place something else (e.g., a plate) flat down.

| **To lie** | *Present tenses* | I lie or am lying |
| | *Past tenses* | I *lay* or was lying |
| | | I have *lain* |
| **To lay** | *Present tenses* | I lay it or am laying it down |
| | *Past tenses* | I *laid* it or was laying it down |
| | | I have *laid* it down |

### (b) Shall and will

I/we *shall*, you/he/they *will* are the simple future tense.

I/we *will*, you/he/they *shall* express a strong wish or determination:

e.g. They *shall* not pass. I *will* not give in.

(Note: *Will* is now commonly used for all persons in the simple future tense.)

### (c) May, might, can

*Can* means *to be able to*.
*May* is the present tense; *might* is the past tense.

(Both mean *to be permitted*.)

*May* also expresses a distinct possibility: *might* expresses the idea that it is just possible but unlikely.

### (d) Each other and one another; between and among

*Each other* and *between* refer to two people or things; *one another* and *among* refer to more than two:

e.g. In the duel they hurt *each other*.
The boys in the class were fighting *one another*.

### (e) Like and as

*Like* is a preposition (or an adjective) but not a conjunction. It should not be followed by a finite verb. Use *as* if you mean *in the same way that:*

**Wrong:**  He talks like I do.
**Right:**   He talks *as* I do.

### (f) Past and passed

Use *passed* for the verb (and its past participle); *past* for all other uses:

e.g. He passed me the ball. He has passed.
in the past (noun); he went past (adverb); in past ages (adjective); he ran past me (preposition).

### (g) Of, off, have

**Wrong:**  I must of made a mistake.
**Right:**   I must *have* made a mistake.
(*Of* is not a verb.)

*Of* means belonging to or relating to. *Off* means away from or down from a place:

e.g. He fell off the cliff.

## (h) Should and would

The main uses are:

    **(i)** *Should* or *would* is used (depending on the person) as part of another verb expressing the future in the past:

        e.g. I/we *should* be glad . . .
            you/he/she/they *would* be glad . . .

    **(ii)** *Should,* used with all persons, also means *ought to:*

        e.g. I/you/they *should* be playing on the team.

    **(iii)** *Should,* also with all persons, is used for *if* clauses:

        e.g. If you should see him, give him my regard.

    **(iv)** *Would,* with all persons, also expresses the idea of willingness:

        e.g. I *would* play if I could.

    **(v)** *Would,* with all persons, can also mean *used to:*

        e.g. As a child he *would* play for hours.

## 11 Mixed constructions

### (a) Faulty comparisons

**Wrong:** as good if not better than ...
**Right:** as good as if not better than ...
   **or:** at least as good as ...

### (b) Double negatives

**Wrong:** I don't want nothing.
**Right:** I don't want anything.
   **or:** I want nothing.

**Wrong:** He couldn't hardly believe it.
**Right:** He could hardly believe it.

### (c) Hardly/scarcely, when they mean *no sooner ... than,* are followed by *when* (or *before*), not *than:*

e.g. He had hardly/scarcely written a page when/before the bell rang.

### (d) Mixed tenses

**Wrong:** I should be glad if you will ...
**Right:** I should be glad if you would ...
   **or:** I shall be glad if you will ...

**Wrong:** I have and always will be a football fan.
**Right:** I have been, and always will be, a football fan.

**Wrong:** I didn't ought to have done it.
**Right:** I ought not to have done it.

## (e) Order of adjectives

**Wrong:** the three first chapters (there is only one *first* chapter)
**Right:** the first three chapters (meaning chapters one, two and three)

## (f) Try to/try and...

Normally use try *to,* except when you mean two separate actions:

e.g. Try to aim high or you may try and fail.

## (g) Between is followed by *and* (not *or*):

e.g. He had a choice between baseball *and* tennis.

## (h) Comprise (meaning *consist of, be composed of*) does not need *of:*

e.g. The kit comprised (or was composed of) four items.

## (i) Don't repeat a preposition

**Wrong:** These are the subjects to which he must pay attention to.

## (j) Them/those

**Wrong:** Give me them slippers.
**Right:** Give me those slippers.

## 12   Misused words

**(a) Literally** means exactly to the letter, in actual fact.

**Wrong:**   He literally flew down the street. (He didn't sprout wings.)

**(b) Unique** means the only one of its kind — like the phoenix. Strictly, things can't be quite unique or very unique. (Likewise with *invaluable* [meaning priceless].)

**(c) etc.** This is an abbreviation of *et cetera*, meaning "and the rest." It should not be used lazily; specify what you have in mind. Don't write *and etc.*, *ect.* or *e.t.c.*

## 13   Redundancy/Wordiness

**Wrong:**   He is equally as clever as his brother.
**Right:**   He is as clever as his brother.

**Wrong:**   He fell off of his horse.
**Right:**   He fell off his horse.

**Wrong:**   The reason why is because . . .
**Right:**   The reason is that . . .
  **or:**   This is because . . .

**Wrong:**   Long ago since . . .
**Right:**   Long since . . .

**Wrong:**   You're nearer my age than what she is.
**Right:**   You're nearer my age than she is.

*Assemble, cooperate, mix* and *mingle* do not normally require the word *together*.

*Meet* is to be preferred to *meet up with* and *miss* to *miss out on*.

Avoid *seeing as* — use *as* or *since*.

Use *just* or *exactly,* but not both.

*But* does not need *however, yet* or *nevertheless*.

*As to* is often used unnecessarily, especially before *whether*.

Avoid needless repetition such as *advance* planning, *close* proximity, *end* result, *grateful* thanks, *habitual* custom, *local* resident, *mutual* cooperation, *old* adage, *past* history, return *back, self*-confessed, *successful* achievements, *true* facts, *usual* customs, and *young* teenager.

Use *now* rather than "at this moment in time" or "at the present"

> *because* rather than "on the grounds that" or "owing to the fact that"
>
> *if* rather than "in the event that"
>
> *soon* rather than "at an early date"
>
> *since* rather than "owing to the fact that"
>
> *early* rather than "ahead of schedule"
>
> *have* rather than "am in possession of"
>
> *today* rather than "in this day and age"
>
> *was* rather than "had occasion to be"
>
> *thought* rather than "was of the opinion that"

## 14  Mixed metaphors

These occur when you are not thinking and particularly when you are using overworked metaphors.

e.g.  The policeman ironed out the bottleneck. (Try it!)

## 15   **Ambiguity** (confusion of meaning)

This is often caused by:

**(a)** unclear pronouns:

e.g. She likes me more than you.
     This could mean
     *either:* She likes me more than she likes you.
       *or:* She likes me more than you do.

Generally, ask yourself if it is clear to whom or what the pronoun refers, especially when you are using *it* or *they,* and *as* or *than*.

**(b)** wrong punctuation or word order:

e.g. The door opened and a young woman carrying a baby and her husband entered.

(See also subsections 3 and 8 above.)

## 16   **Words overworked or loosely used**

**(a)** *Nice, good, bad, lovely, fine, real, get*.

Overusing any word can cause monotony and blunt meaning, but the above are usually too vague or loosely colloquial for accurate writing, though they can sometimes be used with force. *Get,* though often too colloquial, may at times be the most natural expression. (e.g., He got off the bus.)

Other popular words which are loosely used are:

> fantastic, fabulous, tremendous, terrific, great, incredible, diabolical, ghastly, definitely

In general, look for a more precise word.

**(b)** Avoid colloquialisms (expressions from common speech) like *a lot, lots of, a bit* and *kind of* in formal writing.

**(c)** Clichés (i.e., very common overused expressions) such as the following should be avoided:

> an ongoing situation
> accidents will happen
> all things considered
> all too soon
> auspicious moment
> bated breath
> better late than never
> bone of contention
> by leaps and bounds
> clear as crystal
> due consideration
> easier said than done
> goes without saying
> in no uncertain terms
> lend a helping hand
> more than meets the eye
> no way
> powers that be
> scathing sarcasm
> this day and age

**(d)** *Then, so* and *suddenly.* Often casually used or overused by young writers, these words can cause disjointedness and dullness. Give more thought to varied, logical and effective sentence construction.

# 5 Notes on summarizing (précis)

## HINTS ON REDUCING THE LENGTH OF SHORT PASSAGES

The object is to put into your own words, simply and briefly, the essential ideas of the original.

## 1 Generalizing

State the main points clearly, omitting details, examples and illustrations. (If the writer has used examples as his or her *only* means of expressing an important point, "translate" them into a general statement.)

## 2  Recasting sentences

Simplify sentences by making phrases do the work of clauses, and single words the work of phrases. (Omit sentences that merely repeat or illustrate a point.)

## 3  Figurative language

Avoid all figures of speech; express ideas in plain, literal language. Omit illustrative comparisons and contrasts.

## 4  Redundancy and repetition

Cut out unnecessary words and phrases; make a point once only.

# METHOD OF SUMMARIZING LONGER PASSAGES

## 1  Procedure

**(a)** Read through the whole passage to catch its general meaning. Then ask yourself what it is about. (It may help to give it a title.)

**(b)** Carefully re-read the passage, two or three times if necessary, to grasp its exact meaning. (At this stage briefly summarize the writer's basic line of thought.)

**(c)** Note down, in skeleton form, its essential points, paying special attention to the main parts of complex sentences, and to key sentences of paragraphs. (Omit purely illustrative passages.)

**(d)** Memorize these essential points (and the links between them), put the original passage and the notes aside, and do a first draft of the summary *in your own words,* in one paragraph.

**(e)** Revise this first draft, which may well be too long. Prune it of superfluous words and phrases, reconstructing parts of it if necessary. Refer to the passage if you need to, ensuring that you have not "lifted" groups of words from it. Be sure that your version *connects* the ideas correctly (check link words such as *but, therefore*) and that it is not disjointed and telegraphic in style, but reads smoothly like an original composition. Combine sentences to save words, to establish the links between ideas and to achieve fluency.

**(f)** Write the revised copy, stating at the end the number of words it contains.

## 2  Notes

**(a)** Remember that the object is to give a true summary of the original. Add nothing of your own, and do not correct any factual mistakes the original may contain.

**(b)** It is usually advisable to follow the order of the original, but the ideas may be rearranged in any order, if this clarifies their logical sequence.

**(c)** It is not essential to use reported speech (third person and past tense) in every summary, but, if the original is written in the first person, the summary must make clear at the outset that someone else's views are being reported.

**(d)** The same techniques apply to a summary of particular topics contained *within* a passage. Pay careful heed to what is required before sifting the points.

# 6 Essays and compositions

## SOME DOS AND DON'TS

### Do:

**(a)** plan your material (on scratch paper) and decide on the best approach and treatment

**(b)** keep to the subject and make your meaning clear

**(c)** develop the theme of each paragraph and link each paragraph to the following one

**(d)** work out your sentences mentally before writing

**(e)** choose words for their accuracy of meaning and aptness to context

**(f)** vary the length and pattern of your sentences

**(g)** give special care to opening and concluding paragraphs, making them as effective as possible

**(h)** be prepared to work over and rewrite certain sections

**(i)** finally, read through carefully, making necessary corrections clearly

## Don't:

**(a)** write what is too obvious or superficial

**(b)** repeat yourself or "ramble"

**(c)** use slang or colloquialisms

**(d)** write disconnected sentences or sketchy paragraphs

**(e)** be unnecessarily pompous or affected

**(f)** use several words where one would do

## SUGGESTIONS FOR DIFFERENT TYPES OF COMPOSITION

### 1 Formal essays dealing with ideas, information, arguments

**(a)** First jot down ideas freely for a few minutes, asking yourself plenty of questions.

**(b)** Look for an overall structure and approach: e.g., For and Against.

**(c)** Then sort out the best material under paragraph headings and in a logical sequence.

**(d)** Provide "links" between your paragraphs.

**(e)** Remember that each paragraph is built on *one* main topic and should develop this topic fluently, usually with illustrative detail.

## 2    Descriptive and imaginative prose

**(a)** Train yourself to observe in a lively, accurate, honest way.

**(b)** Try to make the reader see, feel, hear, and believe in the impressions you create.

**(c)** Use your imagination to perceive fresh likenesses (e.g., through metaphor and simile).

**(d)** Be economically suggestive — select only the most telling details.

**(e)** Choose words for the aptness of their associations and tone as well as for their precise meaning.

**(f)** Arrange your material to achieve *unity* of atmosphere, mood, or viewpoint.

**(g)** Shape the rhythm and pattern of your sentences to your purpose.

## 3 Stories and character portraits

**(a)** Work out a clear story line with a logical sequence of events. Don't pack in too many sensational incidents or follow conventional, hackneyed plots. It is often best to concentrate on a few centers of interest and on one climax, and explore fully the imaginative possibilities of these. Consider various different methods of telling your story — by first-person narrative, flashback, etc.

**(b)** Vivid, detailed descriptions of place, weather, etc., will help to create a convincing setting (and atmosphere) for your story. Sharp observation will help to make it real.

**(c)** Dialogue may help to create drama and atmosphere or illustrate character, but it can easily become flat unless you concentrate upon the feelings and reactions of the individual characters. Dialogue should, of course, suit character.

**(d)** Try to put yourself in the shoes of all your characters, considering their motives, feelings, reactions, and the interaction between characters. (It may help to start with a description of a person's physical appearance and then let character emerge through action and dialogue.)

**(e)** Once again, you need an overall design that integrates all the parts.

## 4   Research papers

**(a)** Research and notes: Find as much relevant material as you can from books, periodicals, journals, etc. (Check the table of contents and index.) Make notes (see Chapter 7) as you read, using headings and subheadings and putting direct quotations in quotation marks.

**(b)** Planning and writing: Make a careful plan of your main line of argument or ideas, organizing your material in a logical sequence. Avoid vagueness, wordiness, and sweeping generalizations; instead, develop your ideas clearly and fully, supporting them with evidence.

**(c)** Acknowledging sources: Acknowledge your sources either by reference to the author/work or by direct quotation. This can be done either within the text or in footnotes, for which you should use a numbering system in the text and give the source at the bottom of the page or at the end of the chapter. Add a bibliography at the end, listing all works used or quoted from.

## HINTS ON TAKING EXAMINATIONS INVOLVING IMPROMPTU ESSAYS

**(a)** By the time of the examination you should know what *kind* of composition you normally write best (and worst!), e.g., narrative, descriptive, argumentative.

**(b)** After reading the questions carefully and thinking of interesting, original ways of treating them, make a *firm* choice; then forget about the others.

**(c)** Plan on scratch paper, concentrating on finding a fresh, lively, personal approach, on developing and illustrating ideas, on building up a detailed and coherent imaginative picture. (Check for *relevance*. Avoid writing in slang or dialect.)

**(d)** Plan for about six paragraphs of roughly equal length for an essay of 450-500 words. Paragraphs that seem likely to be "thin" or disjointed should be scrapped or worked over.

**(e)** Before writing, make sure your essay has unity of design; you may need to rearrange material or to provide links between paragraphs.

**(f)** Always leave time to correct your work.

## GENERAL

Remember that most people write best about their personal experiences and that freshness and originality of approach are what make writing interesting and distinctive. Where possible, be yourself.

(The above notes are obviously no substitute for creative experiment, for the rich stimulus of good literature, and for constant practice.)

# 7 Notetaking and notemaking

These are essential skills for all students.

**(a)** The best notes are usually *short*.

**(b)** Note only *important* points or facts.

**(c)** Use *keywords* and *key phrases*.

**(d)** *Lay out* the notes usefully (a page with half-a-dozen spaced-out key phrases may be better remembered and give a clearer sense of structure than a block of twenty lines of solid writing).

**(e)** *Read through* and, if possible, *pare down* the notes *immediately* after taking them.

**(f)** Picture or "flow diagram" notes may be used in any subject because they

    **(i)** are *easier to memorize*.

**(ii)** are *easily referred to*.

**(iii)** can show immediately the *relationship* between topics, events, ideas.

**(iv)** allow one to explore topics, further, investigating new links between the key issues, arriving at new understandings.

(They may also be used *actively* — i.e., for problem-solving, creative thinking, essays.)

## Using reference books

Scan with a pencil, ruler, bookmark. With practice this aids both concentration and memorizing. A suggested procedure is:

**(a)** Check contents, index; look over the first and last chapters — the last chapter may be a summary of the book.

**(b)** Look over your selected sections, especially the first and last sentences of paragraphs, diagrams, tables, etc.

**(c)** Now look closely at the text, making your notes.

**(d)** (very important) Go over your notes immediately after you have finished. Reject the unnecessary.

## Memorizing

To memorize notes, theorems, quotations, etc., try to write out the information *from memory* and then compare what you have written with the original notes. After notes and check-through have been made, revision should take place after an hour, then a week, then a month, or at similar intervals as convenient.

# 8  Formal letters

Letter-writing is a branch of good manners. You will often be judged on the letters you write — to prospective employers, for instance. The following notes apply to formal or official letters.

## 1  Paper

It is important to use *good,* preferably *white, unlined* paper. It is always best to rough out your letter first — it can serve as your reference copy — as this will help you avoid mistakes, save expensive notepaper and give you an idea of the spacing and layout of the letter, enabling you to avoid crossings-out or signing off just over the page. Check your expression, punctuation, and spelling. If you do make a mistake that requires crossing out, scrap the letter and rewrite the whole.

## 2   Addressing envelopes

Envelopes should match the paper.

### (a) Layout

Mr. John Blank                 The Personnel Manager
100 Blank Street               Blankton Company, Inc.
Blankton, NJ 20117             111 First Avenue
                               Blankton, NY 11791

Write a legible address with a zip code. (Punctuation at the ends of lines is not necessary.)

### (b) Warnings

Remember that you are writing to a particular person. Use his or her name or office/title:

e.g. The Registrar, The Principal, The Personnel Officer

## 3   The letter

### (a) Layout

Leave a margin space of at least 1½ inches down the left-hand side and at top and bottom, and 1 inch down the right-hand side.

(Your address)  5 Blank Street,
Blankton, NJ 20117

(Addressee)  (Date in full)  July 27, 1990

The Registrar
State University
Blankton, MI 48500

Dear Sir or Madam:

. . . . . . . . . . . . . . . . . . . . . . . . . . . . . . . . . . . .
. . . . . . . . . . . . . . . . . . . . . . . . . . . . . . . . . . . .

Yours truly,

(Signature)

Notes on layout:

**(i)** In the sample addresses, the all-capitalized, unpunctuated, two-letter Postal Service state abbreviation was used. It is equally correct to spell out the state name, or to abbreviate it using standard punctuation (e.g., Michigan or Mich.). But remember to be consistent; whatever form is used for your return address should be used for the addressee's address.

**(ii)** Date in full, *not* 7-29-90 or July 29th, etc.

**(iii)** "Yours truly," on the left-hand side below the message. (Notice comma following.)

**(iv)** Beneath this, your signature *legibly* written. (Beneath this, your name typewritten.)

## (b) Mode of address and signing off

If you do not know the name of the addressee, use "Dear Sir or Madam:" If you do know the name of the addressee, use "Dear Mr. Blank:" or "Dear Ms. Blank:" A sign off should be chosen that expresses the appropriate degree of formality or informality (e.g., "Yours truly," would be formal; "Sincerely yours," less formal; "Best regards," less formal still).

## (c) General

In general, aim at clarity, conciseness, and dignity of expression. Be polite and direct. Avoid verbosity and business jargon, as well as colloquialisms, slang, and contractions.

If you are replying to a letter, you should normally first thank the sender thus: "Thank you for your letter of January 16."

Start a new paragraph for your message. (It is common now, particularly in business letters, not to indent the first line of a paragraph. Instead, paragraphs are separated by spaces between them. This is also often done in books that consist of notes rather than continuous text — as this book does.)

When making requests, you will find the following a useful construction: "I would appreciate it if you would..."

When applying for a job, you could use a heading note before the "Dear...": e.g., Subject: Advertisement in *The Daily Globe,* 12-10-90 (the date may be abbreviated in such cases).

In letters of a more friendly nature (not "chatty" letters to the family) you may be more expansive and personal in style, but must judge the *tone* tactfully and adapt sensibly to the demands of the occasion. Think of the impression your letter gives and imagine yourself in the place of the recipient. Have you assumed the right manner? Have you given the information required in a clear, orderly fashion? Have you made your requests clearly? As with all forms of writing, some forethought and planning are needed. (Note: A friendly letter should end with "Best regards," "With best wishes," or something similar — keep your "fun" endings for your close friends and relations.)

# 9 Useful terms

## GRAMMATICAL

Language employs the following units: (**i**) single words, (**ii**) phrases, (**iii**) clauses, (**iv**) sentences, (**v**) paragraphs.

**1 Parts of speech** (i.e., the different jobs done by words)

**(a)** A **noun** names a person, thing or quality:

e.g. boy, John, brick, beauty, decision

**(b)** A **pronoun** stands in place of a noun (to avoid repeating it):

e.g. he, him, me, it, they, them, you, anyone, who, whom

**(c)** a **verb** expresses an action (or state of being):

e.g. he *ran,* he *is . . . ,* I *will go.*
(It has several tenses that show when the action takes place.)

**(d)** An **adjective** describes a noun (or pronoun). It can either stand in front of a noun or refer back to it:

e.g. a *black* cat; *my own* work; the *quick brown* fox; the street is *long*

**(e)** An **adverb** usually "modifies" a verb, telling how, where, when or why an action is done. It can also modify an adjective or another adverb. Except for very common ones, adverbs usually end in *-ly.*

e.g. He ran *quickly.* (*quickly* modifies the verb *ran*)
*very* good (*very* modifies the adjective *good*)
*extremely* well (*extremely* modifies the adverb *well*)

**(f)** A **conjunction** joins, or shows the relationship between, words, phrases, or clauses (see 5(b) below):

e.g. ham *and* eggs; poor *but* honest; for better *or* for worse; he played well, *although* he was injured.

**(g)** A **preposition** introduces a phrase and is followed by a noun or pronoun (which it "governs"):

e.g. Put it *on* the table; *by* air; *up* the pole; *over* the hills; *between* you and me

**(h)** An **interjection** is an exclamatory word (or phrase). It can be taken out of the sentence without destroying the sense:

e.g. *Well, er, no, oh dear, ugh!*

## Nouns and Pronouns as "Subject," "Direct Object," and "Complement"

The **subject** is the person or thing doing the action (or being something):

e.g. *Jack* built the house. *He* hit me. *She* was a nurse.

The **direct object** is the person or thing affected by the action. (It answers the question "Whom?" or "What?")

e.g. Jack built *the house*. (The object — *house* — is what he built.)
He hit *me*.

*The* **complement** completes the sense of verbs like *to be, to become,* and *to seem:*

e.g. He is *an actor.*

The **personal pronouns** in the nominative (subjective) case are as follows (the objective — accusative — case pronouns are given only where they differ):

|              | **Singular**          | **Plural**     |
|--------------|-----------------------|----------------|
| *1st person* | I (me)                | we (us)        |
| *2nd person* | you                   | you            |
| *3rd person* | he/she/it (him/her)   | they (them)    |

## 2 Phrases

A phrase is a group of words (two or more) that acts as a noun, adjective, or adverb:

e.g. *To write well* requires practice. (The italicized phrase acts as a noun, "subject" of the verb *requires*.)

The boy *wearing the blue vest* came second. (Adjective phrase describing the noun *boy*.)

Put it *on the table*. (Adverb phrase, telling where the action is to be done.)

## 3 Simple sentences

A simple sentence contains one finite verb, i.e., a verb used with its subject. The subject, in person and number, determines the form of the verb:

e.g. John *sings* well.

(A finite verb may consist of several verbs that make up its tense:

e.g. John *should have been playing,* but he was ill.)

## 4 Clauses

A clause is a group of words containing a finite verb. There are two basic types:

**(a) Main clause** – the "backbone" of the sentence. It often makes a simple sentence on its own (but see noun clauses below).

**(b) Subordinate clause** – this, like a phrase, acts as an adjective, adverb or noun, and depends upon the main clause.

## 5 Types of subordinate clauses

### (a) Adjective clause

e.g. The man *who called yesterday* must have been a salesman. (The italicized words describe *the man*.)
I found the book *(that) I had been searching for.* (Describes *book*.)
He was absent on the day *when it happened*. (Describes *day*.)

### (b) Adverb clause

There are various kinds:

#### (i) Time

e.g. The crowd cheered *when the President appeared*. (When?)

### (ii) Place:

e.g. He hid the gold *where no one would find it*. (Where?)

### (iii) Reason:

e.g. He won *because he had more stamina*. (Why?)

### (iv) Purpose:

e.g. He worked hard *so that he would pass his exam*. (With what intention?)

### (v) Result:

e.g. They played so well *that they won the cup.* (With what result?)

### (vi) Condition:

e.g. You will succeed *if you try hard*. (On what condition?)

### (vii) Concession:

e.g. *Although they played well,* they still lost. (In spite of what?)

### (viii) Manner:

e.g. They did *as they pleased*. (How?)

### (ix) Degree (or comparison):

e.g. He sings better *than I do*. (To what extent? Compared with what?)

**(c)** The **noun clause** may

    **(i)** be the **subject** of the main verb:

        e.g. *Why he did it* remains a mystery.

    **(ii)** be the **direct object** of the main verb:

        e.g. I do not know *whether he will come*.

    **(iii)** be the **complement** of a verb of being:

        e.g. This is *how we do it*.

    **(iv)** be **in apposition to** a previous noun or pronoun (i.e., enlarging upon or restating it):

        e.g. The idea *that he could be guilty* never crossed our minds.
        It never crossed our minds *that he was guilty*.

    **(v)** follow a **preposition:**

        e.g. The point of *what he said* eludes me.
        He gave an account of *when it happened*.

In all the above examples in **(a), (b)** and **(c),** the words *not* italicized form the main clause.

A sentence containing a main clause and one or more subordinate clauses is called a **complex** sentence. A sentence containing two or more main clauses (joined by *and, but, or*) is called a **compound** sentence; it may also contain subordinate clauses.

## 6 Paragraphs

A paragraph is a set of sentences (sometimes just one) developing *one* topic. (Make sure you indent the first line clearly, but see Chapter 8, subsection 3(c) for letters.)

## 7 Non-finite verb forms

These are *incomplete* forms.

**(a)** The **infinitive:**

e.g. *to walk, to be considered, to have seen*

**(b) Participles.** The present participle ends in *-ing;* the past in *-ed* (usually).

A participle may

> **(i)** act as an adjective:
>
> > e.g. a *talking* doll
>
> **(ii)** introduce an adjective phrase:
>
> > e.g. *Talking* very loudly, they got on the train.
>
> **(iii)** help form a finite verb with other verb parts:
>
> > e.g. I had been *talking* to him.

**Note:** the *-ing* ending may denote a gerund (a *noun*):

e.g. *Talking* is forbidden.

## 8   Active and passive

When the subject is performing the action, the verb is said to be in the "active voice":

e.g. Jack *built* the house.

When the subject is suffering the action, the verb is said to be in the "passive voice":

e.g. The house *was built* by Jack.

## 9   Transitive and intransitive verbs

A **transitive** verb takes an object:

e.g. He woke *his brother*. She boiled *an egg*. (Objects italicized.)

An **intransitive** verb does not:

e.g. He awoke. The water boiled.

## 10   Indirect objects

The indirect object is the person (or thing) *to* or *for* whom the action is done:

e.g. Pass the ball to *him*. He gave *me* a book. (*me* means *to me*.)

## 11 Prefixes

A prefix is a small group of letters (often from Latin or Greek) put at the beginning of a word to alter its meaning:

e.g. *mis*fire; *anti*aircraft; *extra*ordinary

## 12 Suffixes

A suffix is a group of letters attached to the end of a word to change its function or its meaning:

e.g. The suffix *-ly* turns an adjective into an adverb: *careful* (adjective) becomes *carefully* (adverb).

e.g. *wright* (meaning *workman*) as in *wheelwright* and *playwright*

# LITERARY

An **allegory** is a story that carries another and deeper meaning; the story stands for or suggests something else:

e.g. *The Rime of the Ancient Mariner* is an allegory about guilt.
*Animal Farm* is a political allegory.

(An allegory is a longer version of a parable.)

**Alliteration** is the repeating of sounds (usually consonants at the beginnings of words) to echo the sense or sound of the thing described:

e.g. the stuttering rifle's rapid rattle...
　　 The fair breeze blew, the white foam flew,
　　 The furrow followed free;...

(**Assonance** is repeating vowel sounds for a similar purpose.)

An **allusion** is a brief, often indirect, reference to another literary work or to a person, event, or myth.

**Ambiguity,** used as a literary term, is expressing two or more relevant but different meanings at the same time.

A **ballad** is a poem or folk song that tells a story, often in a dramatic form. The usual ballad has four-line stanzas with four stressed beats in the first and third lines and three in the second and fourth.

e.g. "Sir Patrick Spens" and *The Rime of the Ancient Mariner*

**Blank verse** is unrhymed verse. Each line has ten syllables, the stress tending to fall on every second syllable. (Such a meter is called iambic pentameter.)

e.g. Was this the face that launched a thousand ships
　　 And burnt the topless towers of Ilium?

A **conceit** is an ingeniously developed, often surprising, image or comparison.

A **couplet** is a pair of rhyming lines:

e.g. So long as men can breathe, or eyes can see,
So long lives this, and this gives life to thee.

**Diction** is the choice, use, and arrangement of words in a literary work.

An **elegy** is a formal poem of lament for the dead:

e.g. Gray's "Elegy Written in a Country Churchyard"

An **epic** is a long narrative poem (or other work) about heroic achievements. It is grand in style and scale.

e.g. Milton's *Paradise Lost*, Melville's *Moby Dick*

A **euphemism** is a mild or indirect way of describing an unpleasant or embarrassing thing:

e.g. He passed away.

**Foot/feet;** the sound-unit, of two or three syllables, that is repeated in a line of verse. (See meter)

A **genre** is a form or type of literature:

e.g. tragedy, comedy, epic poetry, science fiction, the short story

**Hyperbole** is exaggeration for effect:

e.g. It took *ages*.

**Imagery** creates vivid pictures or sensations in the mind by likening one thing to another; it includes metaphors and similes. (A poem may be an extended image or set of images.)

**Irony**

>   **(i) Verbal** — when you mean the opposite of what the words state:
>
>   e.g. You're a nice one!
>
>   Antony in *Julius Caesar* calls Caesar's assassins "honorable men" but means the opposite.
>
>   **(ii) Dramatic** — When the audience knows something that one or all of the characters on the stage don't know.

A **lyric** is a song or short poem expressing direct personal feeling:

e.g. Wordsworth's "I Wandered Lonely As a Cloud"

A **metaphor** is a condensed simile (without the word *like* or *as*). One thing is said to *be* the other thing with which it is compared.

e.g. The train *snaked* its way up the valley.
 That boy is a *tiger.*

**Meter** is the rhythmic pattern and length of a line of verse. It consists of a number of metrical "feet." The commonest of these are: iambic, where an un-stressed syllable is followed by a stressed one, e.g., ăgáin; and trochaic, where a stressed syllable is followed by an unstressed one, e.g., thōusănd.

A line with five feet is called a **pentameter:**

e.g. The curfew tolls the knell of parting day.

A line with four feet is called a **tetrameter:**

e.g. The ice was here; the ice was there.

An **ode** is a lyric poem in honor or praise of something. It is usually exalted in style and feeling.

e.g. Keats's "Ode on a Grecian Urn"

**Onomatopoeia** is using words which, through their own *sound,* imitate or suggest the sound of what they describe:

e.g. meow, buzz; the blare of trumpets; the murmur-ing of innumerable bees

A **paradox** is a saying that seems to contradict itself; its apparent nonsense, however, emphasizes a truth:

e.g. More haste, less speed.


A **persona** is a character and voice adopted by an author:

e.g. the Duke in Browning's "My Last Duchess"


**Personification** is treating an abstract quality (like Justice or Honor) as if it were human:

e.g. Hope had grown gray hairs.

It is also commonly used to endow nonhuman things with human feelings:

e.g. The kettle sang merrily.

(**"Pathetic fallacy"** is ascribing human feelings to Nature:

e.g. the angry winds, the kind old sun.)


A **pun** is a play on words, either on two meanings of the same word, or on words sounding alike:

e.g. Drilling holes is *boring*.
     Was King Kong the original urban *guerrilla?*

**Satire** is a work that holds vice or folly up to ridicule:

e.g. *Gulliver's Travels* is a satire on man's pride.

A **simile** brings out a point (or points) of likeness between two different things. It is usually introduced by the word *like* or *as:*

e.g. Her skin was *as white as snow.*
His hand was trembling *like a leaf.*

A **soliloquy** is a speech in a play in which a character thinks aloud while alone on stage:

e.g. Hamlet's "To be or not to be" speech.

A **sonnet** is a fourteen-line poem in iambic pentameter with an elaborate rhyme scheme.

A **stanza** is a regular grouping of rhymed verse, used as a kind of verse paragraph.

A **symbol** is an object (or set of objects) standing for some idea:

e.g. The *cross* is the symbol of Christianity.

The **theme** is the underlying idea, subject, or issue that the writer treats:

e.g. *The Great Gatsby* treats the theme of the American Dream.

**Tone** is the writer's manner of speaking or attitude towards his or her subject and/or reader. (This might be sarcastic, flippant, bitter, etc.)

A **tragedy** is a play (or other work) that describes great suffering and catastrophe in a way that moves us to pity and horror:

e.g. *King Lear*

# Index

# Notes

# Notes

# Notes

# Notes